THE

Marilyn

ALBUM

THE
Marilyn
ALBUM

NICKI GILES

GALLERY BOOKS
An imprint of W.H. Smith Publishers Inc.
112 Madison Avenue
New York, New York 10016

CONTENTS

Published by Gallery Books
A Division of W H Smith Publishers Inc.
112 Madison Avenue
New York, New York 10016

Produced by
Brompton Books Corp.
15 Sherwood Place
Greenwich, CT 06830

ISBN 0-8317-5743-4

Printed in Hong Kong

10 9 8 7 6 5 4 3 2 1

INTRODUCTION

When Marilyn Monroe died on August 4th, 1962 she was 36 years old. She died as she had lived, in the glare of publicity, and it might equally well have been said of Marilyn, as it was of the Beatles, that she was 'more famous than Jesus.' But for all that she led her life and met her death in the limelight, Marilyn remains strangely elusive.

This aura of mystery was at least partly contrived, perhaps unintentionally, by Marilyn herself. One bewildered researcher described her biography as a 'pathological detective story.' This problem arose from Marilyn's habit of changing the details of her early life from one interview to the next. Such embroidery of the facts was less a conscious attempt to deceive than a lifelong attempt to escape from the rejection and instability of her childhood. Indeed, her whole life can be seen as her attempt perpetually to reinvent herself. She married not one but two American legends, in completely different areas of endeavor – Joe DiMaggio, the baseball hero, and Arthur Miller, author of some of the 1950s' most powerful plays, such as *The Crucible* and *All My Sons*, as well as the story of his life with Marilyn, *After the Fall*.

And yet, in becoming all things to all men, Marilyn had nothing left for herself. Director Fritz Lang said of her 'Poor Marilyn was a scared girl, scared of everything. God knows why she was so frightened.' With the benefit of hindsight we can perhaps see that Marilyn was fated, that being plummetted from an unstable childhood into adulation and stardom was too much for Marilyn's mercurial temperament. In the end, Marilyn's enduring memorial will be not the tragedies of her life nor the enigma of her death, but the exhilaration of her life and her screen presence. For men she was the quintessential screen goddess; for women, because of the comedy and vulnerability she projected behind the fabulous façade, she seems a precious vessel of fragile femininity in a ruthless world. For posterity, she remains simply the ultimate movie star.

Right: A youthful Marilyn produces a delightful smile for the camera.

Right: Marilyn on a photographic assignment, probably in the early 1950s.

Left: Beauty and brains! Marilyn in an early publicity shot. Her reading matter includes *Angina, Pectoris and Coronary Occlusion.*

Above: Marilyn as photographed by Hungarian-born André de Dienes, who shot Marilyn over the Christmas of 1945 – much to the annoyance of her then husband James Dougherty.

Right: After being fired by Twentieth-Century Fox in 1947, Marilyn went back to modeling. Here she poses by the swimming pool at the Racquet Club in Palm Springs, California.

Left: Marilyn's response to unfavorable press comments concerning the revealing dress she wore to collect her Henriette Award for Best Young Box Office Personality – a potato sack. Photographer Earl Theisen' studio shot was seen in newspapers across the States.

This page: Two sides of
Marilyn Monroe – the
youthful and carefree girl
(above) and the vulnerable,
self-doubting woman (left).

Right: Marilyn and her third husband, playwright Arthur Miller. Marilyn seems blissfully unaware of the camera; Miller much more wary.

Left: Two Hollywood blondes – Marilyn and Betty Grable – enjoy a night on the town. They starred together in *How To Marry A Millionaire* (1953).

Above: Marilyn puts the finishing touches to her make-up prior to the premier of *How To Marry A Millionaire*. Her regular make-up man, 'Whitey' Snyder, looks on.

Left: Marilyn in the company of *New York Post* columnist Sidney Skolsky, one of Marilyn's greatest supporters. His syndicated column could make or break budding movie careers.

Left: The kind of glamorous
publicity shot much valued
by Hollywood's movie
moguls.

Above: Marilyn poses with
her co-stars in *The Misfits*
(1961), including Clark
Gable (right), Montgomery
Clift (front left), Eli
Wallach(in cap), and Arthur
Miller, the film's
screenwriter (at top).

Right: Marilyn received a
Golden Globe award from
Rock Hudson in 1962
during the Hollywood
Foreign Press Association's
nineteenth annual dinner.
She was named the World's
Favorite Actress.

From Norma Jeane to Marilyn Monroe

1926-47

At 9.30 am on June 1st, 1926 Norma Jeane Mortensen came into the world in the Los Angeles General Hospital. Her mother, Gladys Pearl Mortensen, had been married before and by the time Norma Jeane was conceived, her second husband had left her. The most likely candidate for Norma Jeane's father is Stanley Gifford, who worked at the film lab where Gladys was a film cutter. Later, when she had become Marilyn Monroe, she would attempt a reconciliation with Gifford, only to be rebuffed.

This rejection was really just the culmination of a loveless childhood. For the first eight years of her life, Norma Jeane was farmed out to foster parents while Gladys saved for a home. Norma Jeane saw her mother only at weekends, and shortly after Gladys had finally made a downpayment on a bungalow for them, she was committed to an insane asylum. Mental illness ran like a sore through Gladys's family, and fear of it was to overshadow Marilyn's whole life.

Following two years in a state orphanage, Norma Jeane found several years of relative stability from age ten to age fifteen, with Grace McKee, a friend of her mother's who became her legal guardian. By the time she was fifteen, Norma Jeane was felt by Grace to be marriageable, and a mutually agreeable match was made between her and local teenager, Jim Dougherty. They were married on June 19th, 1942, shortly after Norma Jeane's sixteenth birthday.

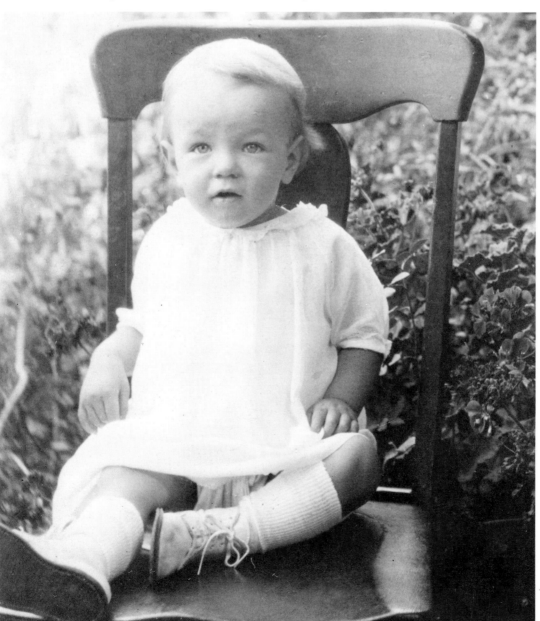

Left: Marilyn as a child. She was born Norma Jeane Mortensen at 9.30 am on June 1st 1926 in the Charity Ward of Los Angeles General Hospital.

Right: Marilyn's mother, Gladys, was prone to bouts of depression and spent spells in mental institutions. Marilyn had several foster parents but was cared for by Grace McKee for most of her early years.

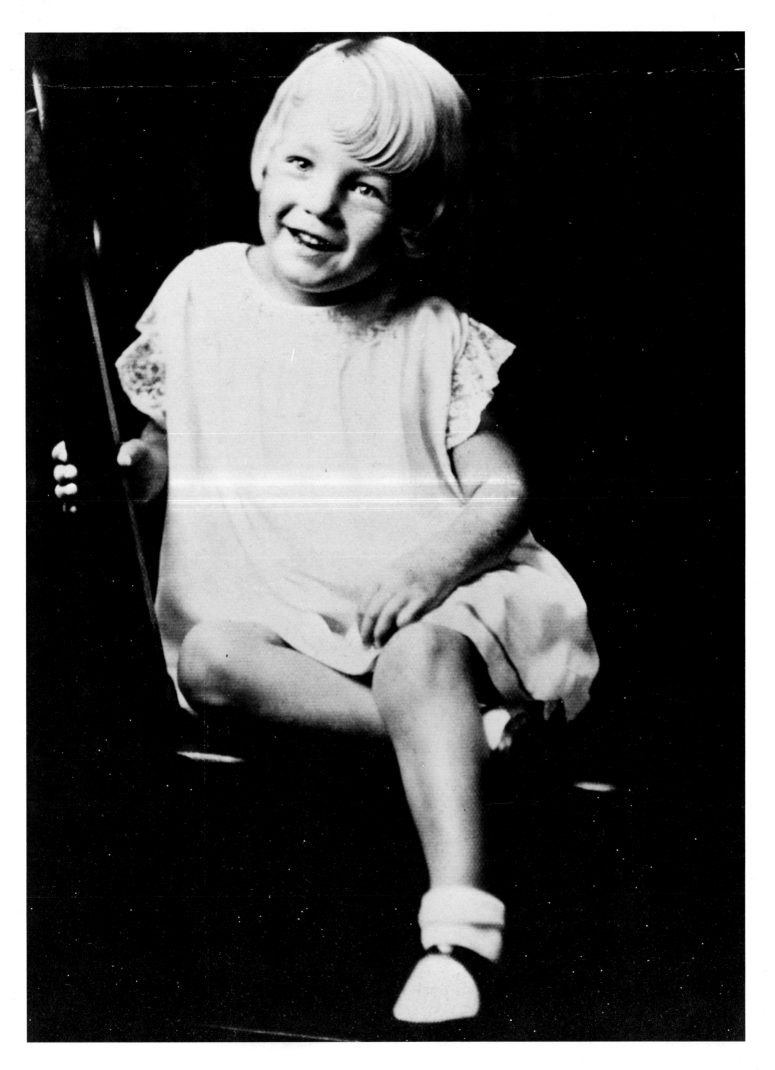

Norma Jeane quickly settled into the routines of homemaking in their own apartment, but soon after their marriage, Jim joined the Merchant Marine. Norma Jeane spent her time going to the movies and dreaming of being a star, but, not surprisingly, she became bored and found herself a job at a local factory.

It was here that the Marilyn story really began. America was at war and an army photographer had been detailed to take morale-boosting shots of women happy in their war work. Private David Conover immediately spotted Norma Jeane and took her picture at work and, in the lunch break, in a clinging red sweater. The June 26th, 1945, issue of *Yank* sported one of these shots and found its way on to the desk of Emmeline Snively, proprietrix of the Blue Book Modeling Agency. Soon Norma Jeane was earning $5 per hour as a freelance model.

With her husband away most of the year and a promising new career opening, Norma Jeane filed for divorce. By 1946 she was on magazine covers everywhere, and Emmeline Snively set up an appointment for her with Ben Lyon, talent scout at Twentieth-Century Fox. The verdict on her screen test was that she had 'flesh impact,' and she was signed up. With her new contract came a new name – Marilyn chosen by Lyon after the stage star Marilyn Miller, and Monroe chosen by Norma Jeane after her grandmother's maiden name.

Marilyn became blonder and had her first walk-on part in *The Shocking Miss Pilgrim* (1947). A film released in the same year, *Dangerous Years*, represented a great leap forward in Marilyn's participation, as she had three lines of dialogue. But most of her first year she spent attending classes in voice production, drama, and movement, or making herself available for cheesecake pictures (sometimes literally, see page 31), and opening supermarkets.

But the path to stardom was not to be straight for Marilyn Monroe, and in August 1947 Twentieth-Century Fox declined to renew her contract. She had, by this time, caught the eye of movie mogul Joe Schenck, who arranged a test for her with Columbia Pictures. They put her under contract and she sang two songs in *The Ladies of the Chorus* (1948). Although she received a favorable review Columbia were not convinced of her abilities and she was dropped. By then she had met several people who were to help and influence the shaping of her career. One was voice coach Fred Karger, with whom she fell hopelessly in love; another was Columbia's head drama coach, Natasha Lytess, with whom Marilyn lived for a while. However, Marilyn had to occupy herself for several months more with her modeling career.

Left: Norma Jeane married Jim Dougherty on June 19th 1942, shortly after her sixteenth birthday. After the ceremony the couple moved into their own apartment and Jim briefly returned to his job with Lockheed Aviation before volunteering to join the Merchant Marine.

Right: Marilyn enjoying the attractions of San Diego Zoo, a picture taken in 1946.

Above: Marilyn flashes a beautiful smile for the camera. Her fresh-faced look enabled her to sign on with Miss Emmeline Snively's Blue Book Modeling Agency shortly after the end of World War II.

Right: Marilyn on an early modeling assignment; the Hollywood glamour image is still some way in the future.

Above: Marilyn in the studio. A picture possibly taken by David Conover, an army photographer who spotted Marilyn while she was working at the local Radio Plane Company. The Seventh Division Medical Corps voted her the girl they would most like to examine.

Far left: One of many shots taken of Marilyn by André de Dienes. Their time together saw them make trips to Las Vegas, the Mojave desert, and Portland, Oregon.

This page: Three early studio shots of Marilyn. On July 19th 1946 Ben Lyon gave Marilyn a screen test at Twentieth-Century Fox. Emmeline Snively had recommended Marilyn to an agent who had links with Lyon. Photographed by Bruno Bernard, this session was a test to advertise first-aid products (visible above left).

Left: Marilyn began her career as an aspiring starlet with an interminable round of publicity shots.

Right: Marilyn models for illustrator Earl Moran in the late 1940s

Above: One of the 'cheesecake' publicity shots produced by film studios for magazines all over the globe. Here, the photographer is Bruno Bernard; the session probably in 1947.

Right and far right: Marilyn at poolside. At right, she is pictured with Johnny Hyde. As Vice-President of the powerful William Morris Agency, he was able to fix up Marilyn's first film roles.

These pages: Marilyn at work, rest, and play in the studio while modeling wear for the skating rink. Taking a break (above, far right), she enjoys a bottle of Coca-Cola while skimming through *Movie News*.

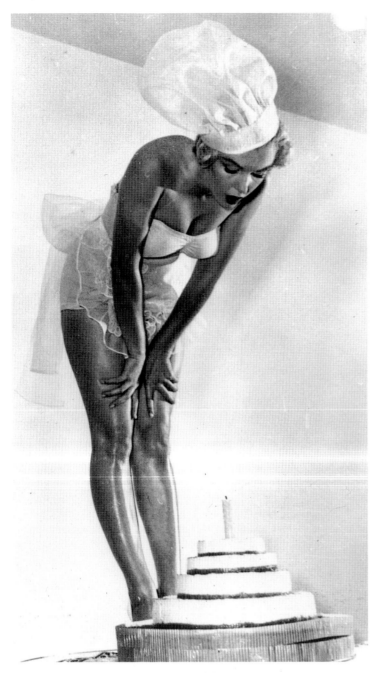

Far left and left: Marilyn modeling a swimming costume and night attire, the latter worn in the 1952 film *We're Not Married*.

Above left and left: Marilyn gets involved in the confectionary business! At left, she poses as 'Miss Cheesecake' with the owner of Michael's Cheesecake Bakery.

Above: Marilyn after getting the full Hollywood treatment. Gone, at least on the surface, is the innocence of youth.

These pages: The changing face of Marilyn Monroe. The effects of Hollywood can be gauged by comparing the picture taken by André de Dienes (below, far right) with the studio shot at left.

The Celluloid Jungle
1948-52

Marilyn's next knight in shining armor arrived in the unlikely shape of Groucho Marx. He needed a walk-on blonde for a Marx Brothers' comedy called *Love Happy*, and Marilyn seemed to fit the bill. For all that she perfected her famous walk in this film, it was followed by a long gap in her film career. It was during this time that Marilyn agreed to pose for the famous nude calendar picture. She had until then always declined to pose nude, believing it would damage her career, but the prospect of the $50 fee was too good to miss in her under-employed state.

Love Happy, although it did not immediately propel her into stardom, did serve to bring Marilyn to the notice of Johnny Hyde of the powerful William Morris Agency. But for his patronage, Marilyn might have been condemned for much longer to appear in such films as *A Ticket to Tomahawk* (1950), in which she coos a lot but has not a single line of dialogue. The diminutive, fast-talking Hyde who had discovered Lana Turner and managed Rita Hayworth, now fell in love with Marilyn Monroe. He believed in Marilyn professionally as well as personally, and secured for her the role of Angela, beautiful 'niece' to a wealthy crooked lawyer. Her performance landed her a role of similar importance in *All About Eve*, directed by Joseph L Mankiewicz. In many ways the part of Miss Caswell in *All About Eve* was typecasting as she is a blonde starlet trying to make her way in a film world peopled by the likes of Bette Davis and George Sanders.

All About Eve brought Marilyn a new contract with Twentieth-Century Fox, but no major film roles for two years, although she did appear in minor parts in ten films between 1950 and 1952. During 1950 Johnny Hyde 'worked' on Marilyn, arranging for her to have her nose and chin slightly altered by plastic surgery, and having her hair regularly bleached. She also had her teeth straightened. When Johnny Hyde died in December 1950, Marilyn attempted suicide by taking

These pages: A variety of poses and a variety of identities offered by Marilyn during the early stages of her first period with Twentieth-Century Fox, probably taken between 1947 and 1948.

sleeping pills. Natasha Lytess arrived in time to avert disaster, but it was a grim premonition of Marilyn's ultimate fate.

Marilyn's first screen drama was *Clash by Night* (1952), in which she made a big impression as Barbara Stanwyck's sister-in-law who envies the older woman's apparent freedom. A bigger impression still was made when the nude-calendar story broke just as filming was finishing. At first the studio was inclined to have her deny her involvement, but faced with the incontrovertible evidence, she admitted it. A suitable story of her needing the $50 to reclaim her repossessed car was cooked up to explain her action, and the publicity did her no harm at all. Soon the 'Golden Dreams' calendar became a collectors' item.

In April *Life* magazine featured her on the cover and called her 'the talk of Hollywood . . . the most talked-about actress in America.' Even so, her next role, as a secretary who cannot type but who can wiggle as she walks, in the film *Monkey Business* (1952), was hardly demanding of her dramatic skills. But it was at this time that Marilyn had her first meeting with America's best-loved baseball hero, Joe DiMaggio. They had dinner and, according to Marilyn, the next night and the next.

For all the glamour and glitter surrounding her relationship and subsequent marriage to DiMaggio, Marilyn was to have several illicit affairs during their time together. This was, of course, unknown to DiMaggio and unknown to her adoring fans. But one skeleton that did emerge from the cupboard of her past was Marilyn's mother Gladys. Studio publicity had always stated that Marilyn was an orphan, but a media hound discovered her mother in a mental institution. Again Marilyn came through this, explaining that her close friends knew her mother was alive and that 'since I have become grown and able to help her, I have contacted her.'

These pages: A series of images that capture Marilyn's beauty and love of life.

Left: Marilyn dressed in a 'fur' bikini.

Right: A publicity shot for Columbia's low-budget musical *Ladies of the Chorus* (1948), Marilyn's first major role.

Above, left to right and right:
Although Marilyn's movie career had
begun by the late 1940s, she was still
available for the usual 'cheesecake'
shots.

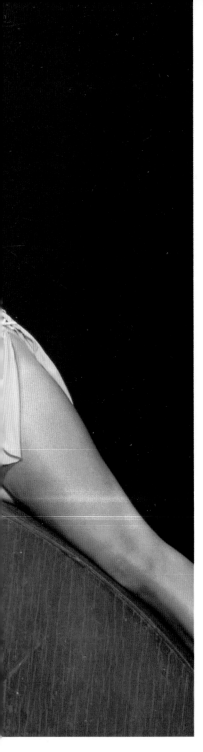

Right: Marilyn had a bit
part in Twentieth-Century
Fox's *Dangerous Years*
(1948), but was dropped by
the studio shortly after
completing the movie.

These pages: *Ladies of the Chorus* was Marilyn's third film, following on from *Scudda Hoo! Scudda Hay!* and *Dangerous Years*. Marilyn sang two songs in the film: 'Everybody Needs A Da Da Daddy' and 'Anyone Can Tell I Love You.'

Above: Marilyn before she was groomed for stardom. While waiting for her big break, she is supposed to have had her teeth straightened.

Above right: Advertising aluminum mounts for photographic transparencies.

Right: Marilyn almost reveals all in yet another publicity shot.

Right: In March 1952 the nude-calendar story broke. After being dropped by Columbia following *Ladies Of The Chorus*, Marilyn, short of funds, posed nude for photographer-friend Tom Kelley.

Left: Marilyn dressed as a 'pilgrim' during a session to promote Thanksgiving Day.

Above left and right, and right: Three photographs of Marilyn, supposedly taken by Earl Moran in 1949.

Posed By **MARILYN MONROE**
In The Nude, With Lace Overprint

These pages: Two views of the nude
Marilyn. They are of course the same,
except for the fact that the one above
has been 'censored' for 'family'
viewing. The Tom Kelley shots were
taken in 1949 but the full story did not
break until 1952. Bravely, Marilyn did
not deny her involvement as her
studio bosses had demanded.

Above and right: By 1950 when these pictures were snapped, Marilyn's career was back on the up. She signed up again for Twentieth-Century Fox that year, and completed six films. Her roles were getting bigger and better.

Far right: Marilyn – the fledgling star.

These pages: *Love Happy* saw Marilyn work alongside the Marx Brothers. Groucho plays a private investigator by the name of Grunion. 'Mr Grunion,' says Marilyn, 'I want you to help me . . . some men are following me.' To which Grunion replies: 'I can't imagine why.'

These pages: The 1950
western musical *A Ticket
To Tomahawk* gave
Marilyn the opportunity to
sing; this time
accompanying the film's
star Dan Dailey as he
croons 'O What A Forward
Young Man You Are.'
Marilyn did not, however,
have a single line of
dialogue.

DAN ANNE
DAILEY BAXTER *in* "**A TICKET TO TOMAHAWK**" *with* A Twentieth Century-Fox Production
RORY CALHOUN WALTER BRENNAN Charles Kemper · Connie Gilchrist · Arthur Hunnicutt · Will Wright · Chief Yowlachie · Victor Sen Yung Cert. "U"
Directed by RICHARD SALE · Produced by ROBERT BASSLER · Colour by TECHNICOLOR · Written by Mary Loos and Richard Sale
This Advertising material is supplied on the express understanding that it will be used for exhibition purposes only, and Not for
Re-sale. Copyright 20th Century-Fox Film Co. Ltd.

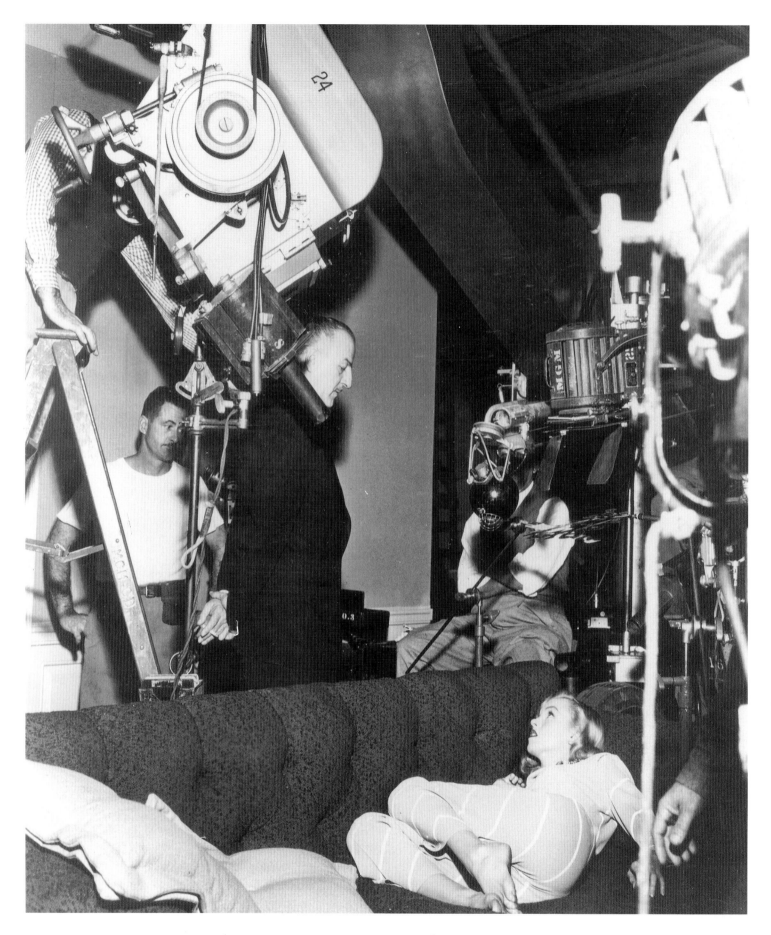

These pages: Marilyn's first big break came with a role in John Huston's classic robbery movie *The Asphalt Jungle* (1950). Marilyn played the 'niece' of a crooked lawyer (Louis Calhern). Movie boss Darryl Zanuck was so impressed by Marilyn's character that he offered her a second contract at Twentieth-Century Fox – this time for seven years.

This page: *All About Eve* (1950) saw Marilyn perform with several leading stars, notably Bette Davis, George Sanders, and Anne Baxter (pictured above). The movie, directed by Joseph L Mankiewicz, won the Oscar for best film. Marilyn's role (two scenes) was limited but her performance was assured.

Right: Mickey Rooney (right), James Brown, and Marilyn enjoy a day out in *The Fireball* (1950). Rooney plays a juvenile delinquent who becomes a ruthless roller-skating champion.

Right: A still taken during the shooting of *Hometown Story* released in 1951. The film extolled the virtues of American industriousness and offered Marilyn little more than the usual cutie-blonde role.

These pages: Following on from *Hometown Story* in 1951, *As Young As You Feel* saw Marilyn play a secretary. Her acting suffered due to the strains brought about by the recent death of Johnny Hyde.

Right: Marilyn promotes *Love Nest* in an advert for 'Rayve Cream Shampoo.' Below: *Love Nest*, released in 1951, was a lightweight comedy scripted by A L Diamond, who would later work with Billy Wilder on *Some Like It Hot*.

Right: Marilyn as a rising star of the early 1950s.

These pages: In *Let's Make It Legal* (1951), Marilyn played a gold-digging blonde. Scripted by A L Diamond, the film starred Macdonald Carey (above, second from left), Claudette Colbert (above, center), and Zachary Scott (above, second from right).

These pages: Fritz Lang's *Clash By Night* (1952) was set in a fishing village and starred Barbara Stanwyck. Marilyn plays Stanwyck's envious sister-in-law in the film and enjoys several scenes with Keith Anders. The film was produced by RKO.

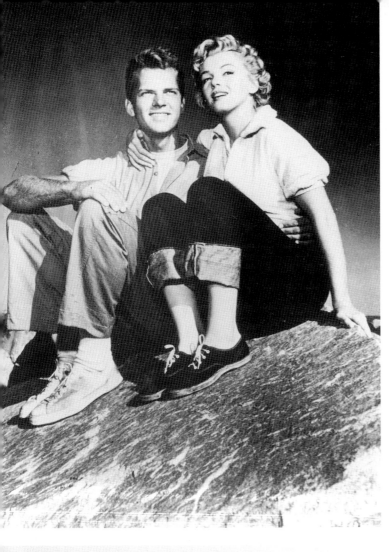

These pages: *Were Not Married* tells
the story of five couples who discover
they are not legally married. Marilyn
plays the role of Annabel who has
just won the 'Mrs Mississippi'
contest, but is barred from entering
the 'Mrs America' contest much to
her husband's delight. Annabel,
however, outwits her 'husband' by
winning the title of 'Miss Mississippi'.
The film was released in 1952.

These pages: The Hollywood publicity machine gets into full swing. Here Marilyn attends a performance of the song 'Marilyn' written by Edwin Drake and Jimmy Shirl in 1952. The routine was performed by band leader Ray Anthony, with a little help from Mickey Rooney (both pictured above left). Her flaming red dress offended many of those present at the poolside ceremony.

These pages: *Don't Bother To Knock* (1952) marked a departure for Marilyn. Working alongside Anne Bancroft and Richard Widmark (above), she played a psychopathic baby-sitter. The film, directed by Roy Baker from a screenplay by Daniel Taradash, was not a great commercial success.

These pages: *Monkey Business* (1952) was directed by Howard Hawks and starred Cary Grant, Ginger Rogers, and Charles Coburn. It is a delightful comedy in which Marilyn plays Miss Laurel, Charles Coburn's dizzy secretary. The plot revolves around a drug which, when taken, regresses everyone to their childhood.

Left: Cary Grant and Marilyn together during the making of *Monkey Business*.

Right and inset right: In *O Henry's Full House* (1952) Marilyn plays the part of a streetwalker opposite Charles Laughton's down-and-out.

PART 3

The Blonde Gentlemen Prefer

1953-55

Marilyn's next big role after the light-weight romp of *Monkey Business*, was *Niagara*. In this dramatically set film Marilyn plays a sizzling *femme fatale* who persuades her young lover to murder her middle-aged husband played by Joseph Cotten. Marilyn gave the character an intriguing undertone of desperation and certainly an erotic potency, which made the other law-abiding characters seem positively bloodless by comparison. *Niagara* was a hit, a fact reflected by the award to Marilyn of the *Redbook* award for Best Young Box Office Personality. From here she moved to a role with which the whole Marilyn ethos seems to be identified, Lorelei Lee in *Gentlemen Prefer Blondes* (1953). Her performance in this film helped secure Marilyn *Photoplay*'s Best Actress award of 1954. Despite the media's best efforts to engineer a feud between Marilyn and her co-star Jane Russell, they seem to have got on fine, and were honored by being asked to add their hand- and footprints to the pavement out-side Grauman's Chinese Theater.

Marilyn was now securing roles in major films with major stars. In *How to Marry a Millionaire* Marilyn, Betty Grable, and Lauren Bacall play three friends who rent a penthouse apartment to ensnare rich husbands for themselves. Marilyn plays a short-sighted girl who for reasons of vanity will not wear her glasses, with comical results. Soon afterwards Betty Grable retired as Fox's #1 blonde, leaving Marilyn to step into her shoes. Just as *Gentlemen Prefer Blondes* proved that Marilyn could look adorable in glasses, so her next film, *River of No Return* revealed that Marilyn could look alluring in jeans.

If her professional life was in need of stimulation, Marilyn's personal life did not lack excitement. On 14 January 1954 she and Joe DiMaggio finally got married after keeping the world waiting for two years. In February they set off on honeymoon for Japan, but when they arrived Marilyn was asked by the US Army to fly to Korea

These pages: Two scenes from *Niagara*. Released in 1953 the movie was directed by Henry Hathaway, and was Marilyn's first major screen part.

These pages: In *Niagara*, Marilyn plays the scheming wife of Joseph Cotten. While holidaying at Niagara Falls, she plots with an infatuated young man to murder her husband. Marilyn was destined to receive the Redbook Award for Best Young Box Office Personality for her role of a *femme fatale* in the film.

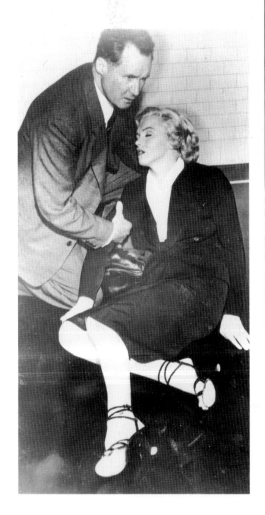

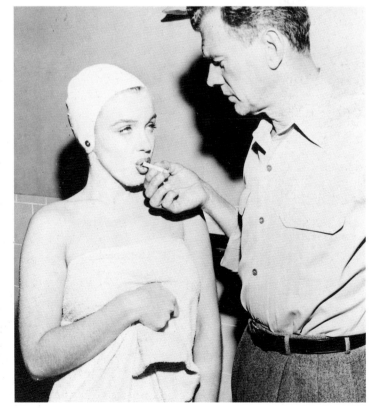

to entertain the troops. The Army was remarkably perceptive in recognizing Marilyn's morale-boosting qualities. She later described the occasion as one of the happiest of her life.

Marilyn was now in a position, if not to choose all her film roles, at least to bargain for those she wanted. For instance, she agreed to take a smallish part in *There's No Business Like Show Business* (1954), in order to land one of her most memorable roles in *The Seven-Year Itch* (1955). No longer did she play an on-the-make blonde, but a girl-next-door (or, rather, upstairs), who also happens to be a blonde bombshell. Tom Ewell plays a summer bachelor who thinks Marilyn is just the girl to scratch his seven-year itch. Over a thousand New Yorkers watched as director Billy Wilder ordered take after take of the famous skirt-blowing scene. Unfortunately the real-life jealous husband, Joe DiMaggio, was watching too. He and Marilyn had been quarreling increasingly about her film roles, and about her public 'performances,' and this was one he could not take. The following month they announced their divorce.

Marilyn Monroe and *Niagara* **the high water mark in suspense!**

Niagara

STARRING

MARILYN MONROE · JOSEPH COTTEN · JEAN PETERS

with CASEY ADAMS · DENIS O'DEA · RICHARD ALLAN

DON WILSON · LURENE TUTTLE · RUSSELL COLLINS · WILL WRIGHT   COLOUR BY *Technicolor*

PRODUCED BY CHARLES BRACKETT   DIRECTED BY HENRY HATHAWAY   WRITTEN BY CHARLES BRACKETT, WALTER REISCH AND RICHARD BREEN

These pages: *Niagara* also contains one of the most famous shots of Marilyn: wearing an impossibly tight-fitting red dress and high heels, she fairly smolders as she performs her 'undulating' walk away from the camera.

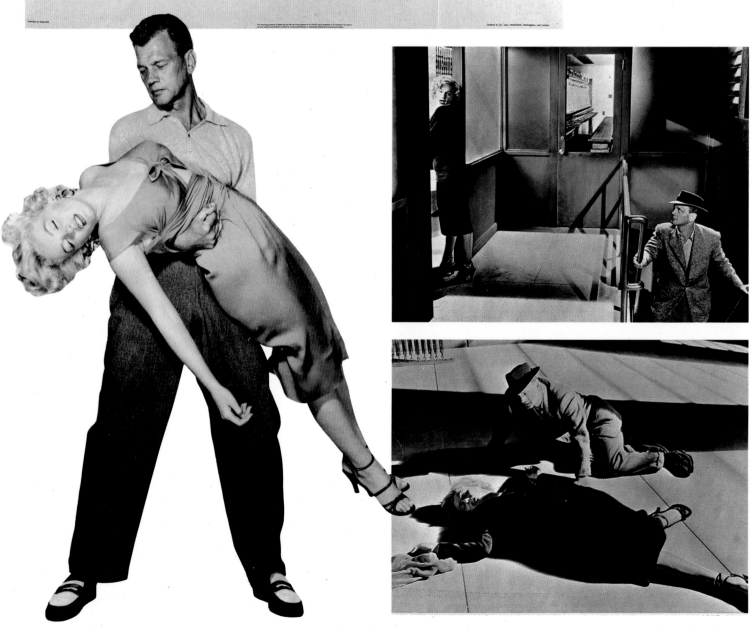

These pages: The role of Lorelei Lee in the screen adaptation of Anita Loos's *Gentlemen Prefer Blondes*, a seemingly witless yet, in fact, a very shrewd baby-faced blonde, was tailor-made for Marilyn. Her co-star for this highly memorable film was Jane Russell.

These pages: Possibly the most famous Marilyn scene ever – 'Diamonds Are A Girl's Best Friend' was the film's show-stopping song-and-dance routine.

Left: Russell and Monroe together. Despite the best efforts of the Press to create a rift between the two, they both appear to have enjoyed working together on the film.

Above and left: Directed by Howard Hawks, *Gentlemen Prefer Blondes* confirmed Marilyn as a rising star. Her salary for the film, allegedly only one-tenth that of Russell, had yet to match her new status.

These pages: *Gentlemen Prefer Blondes* also revealed a darker side of Marilyn's personality. Hawks became increasingly exasperated with his blonde star due to her lack of punctuality.

These pages: Marilyn and Jane, the blonde and the brunette, played a dizzy golddigger and a showgirl in *Gentlemen Prefer Blondes*. Their mission – to find rich husbands in Paris.

Left and above: After vamping up (left), Marilyn captures her husband (above) in *Gentlemen Prefer Blondes*.

Left and below: Two advertisements for *How To Marry A Millionaire*. The film became Marilyn's third hit of 1953.

These pages: Marilyn starred with Betty Grable and Lauren Bacall (see right) in *How To Marry A Millionaire*. The basic story, written by Nunnally Johnson, concerned three friends who rent a penthouse to capture the hearts (and wallets!) of some eligible and wealthy men.

These pages: *How To Marry A Millionaire*, directed by Jean Negulesco, saw Marilyn in the role of a bespectacled blonde who, in order to trap her prospective husbands, would remove her glasses with disastrous results, notably walking into walls.

These pages: Marilyn's performance in *How To Marry A Millionaire* was praised by the Hollywood press. In the company of two acknowledged stars of the caliber of Betty Grable and Lauren Bacall, Marilyn gave a delightful performance. Light musical comedies were clearly her forte.

These pages: Scenes from *How To Marry A Millionaire*. Producer and screenwriter Nunnally Johnson made a telling remark regarding Marilyn: 'It was the first time anybody liked Marilyn for herself.'

These pages: *How To Marry A Millionaire* director Jean Negulesco was somewhat taken aback by Marilyn's lack of confidence during the shooting of the film. On one occasion he reportedly said: 'Marilyn, the only motivation you need for this part is the fact that in this movie you are as blind as a bat without glasses.'

Left: Marilyn waits in her dressing room while the stage crew prepare for her next scene in *How To Marry A Millionaire*.

Right: Studio cop Clyde Cavitt grabs Marilyn's autograph during a break from filming.

Below right: Make-up man 'Whitey' Snyder puts the finishing touches to Marilyn's face during a scene from *How To Marry A Millionaire*.

These pages: Following the comedy *How To Marry A Millionaire* Marilyn played opposite Robert Mitchum in Otto Preminger's thriller *River of No Return*. This film was shot in Canada.

These pages: *River of No Return* saw Marilyn play the role of saloon girl who becomes involved with an ex-jailbird (Mitchum) and his son. The film has plenty of dramatic moments – murder, Indian attacks and roaring rapids. Coincidentally, Marilyn and Mitchum had met before when both he and her first husband Jim Dougherty had worked for Lockheed.

Above: All Aboard! Marilyn gets the locomotive underway to take her to a location in the Canadian Rockies during the filming of *River of No Return*.

Right: Marilyn and Mitchum together. Mitchum was quoted as being less than impressed by his co-star's acting abilities.

Above: Marilyn and a friend at a
preview.

Right: Marilyn models the gold lamé
gown as worn in *Gentlemen Prefer
Blondes*.

These pages: Marilyn pictured with her second husband, the legendary baseball star Joe DiMaggio. Marilyn and Joe married on January 14th, 1954 and divorced in October 1955.

These pages: Marilyn entertains the
troops in Korea. While on honeymoon
in Japan, Marilyn agreed to do 10
shows in Korea. Due to her strenuous
four-day schedule Marilyn contracted
mild pneumonia.

Above: Marilyn and Lauren Bacall
arrive at a Hollywood party in 1954.

Right: Marilyn and Marlon Brando.
They met on the set of Brando's film
Désirée, and rumors abounded of an
affair, though Marilyn strongly denied
them.

These pages: Two pictures from a
photographic assignment in 1954.

These pages: Marilyn worked
alongside Donald O'Connor and Mitzi
Gaynor (above left) in *There's No
Business Like Show Business*, a
cinematic tribute to Irving Berlin,
who wrote the musical score.

These pages: Marilyn was less than happy appearing in *There's No Business Like Show Business*, but put her heart and soul into her two numbers, 'Heat Wave' and 'After You Get What You Want, You Don't Want It.'

These pages: *There's No Business Like Show Business* was directed by Walter Lang and also starred Ethel Merman and Dan Dailey. Its rather thin plot concerned a family of vaudeville performers, The Five Donahues.

These pages: Following the relative
disappointment of *There's No
Business Like Show Business*,
Marilyn's career leapt forward when
she landed the lead role in *The Seven
Year Itch*.

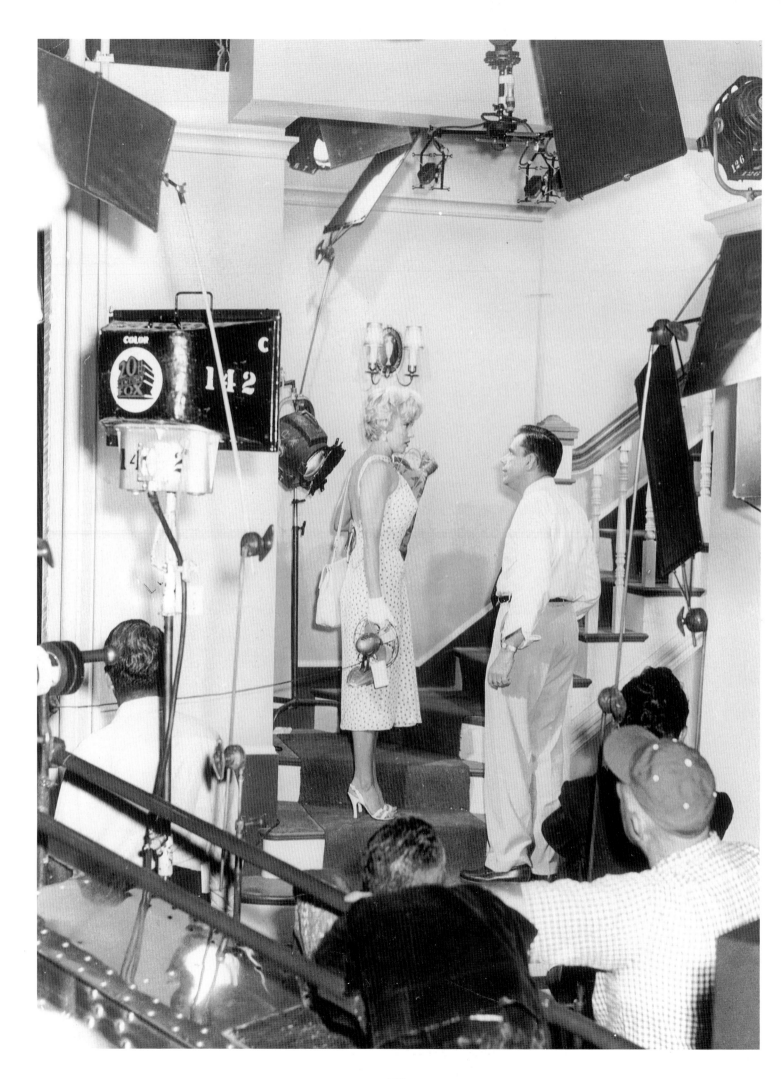

These pages: Marilyn played
opposite Tom Ewell in *The Seven Year
Itch*. Ewell plays a husband left alone
for the summer while his wife and
children are on vacation; Marilyn, a
model and TV commercials actress,
plays the girl upstairs, the object of
Ewell's dreams.

Overleaf: One of the funniest scenes
in *The Seven Year Itch* occurs when
Marilyn gets her big toe stuck in a
bath tap and has to rely on the good
offices of a local plumber to free her
from her predicament.

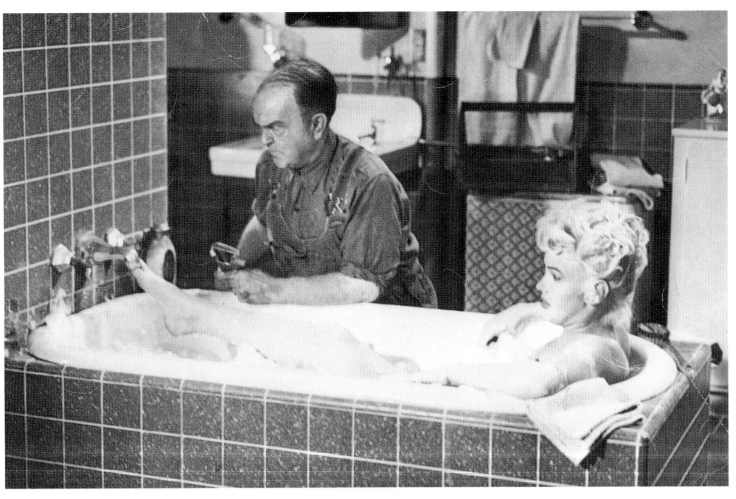

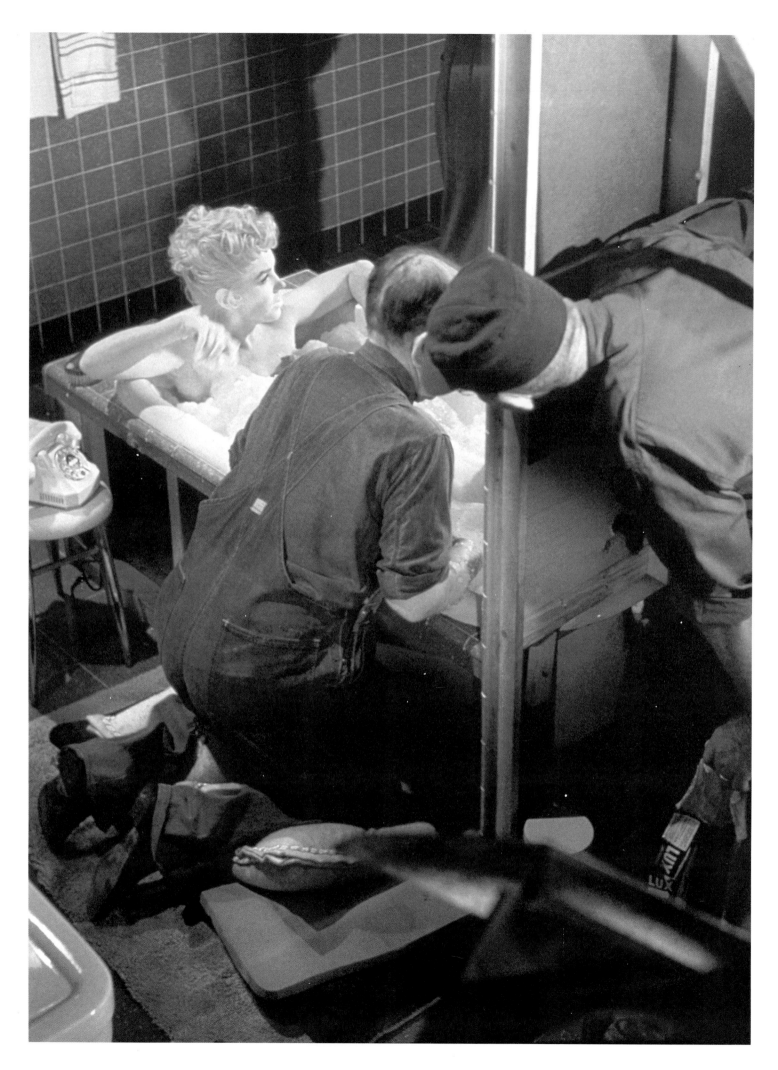

These pages: Marilyn preparing to shoot a couple of scenes from *The Seven Year Itch*.

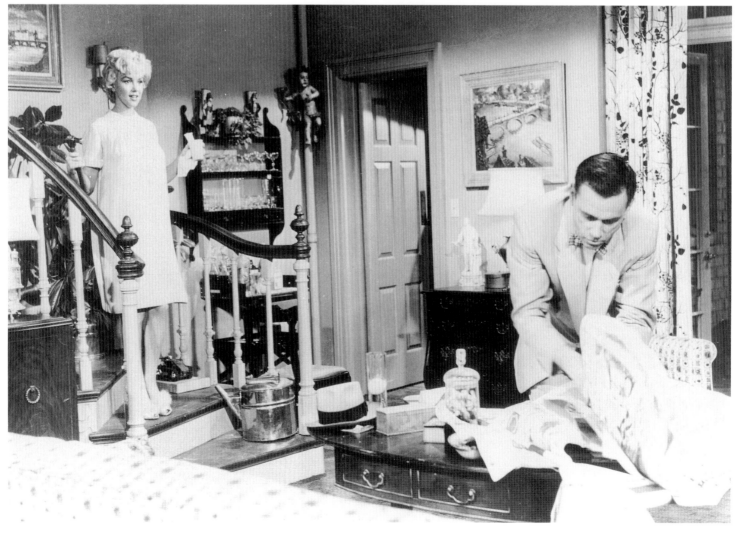

These pages: *The Seven Year Itch* was directed by Billy Wilder for Twentieth-Century Fox; the photographer on the movie was Milton Krasner.

These pages and overleaf: Probably the most famous scene in any Marilyn picture. The skirt-billowing shot was filmed at night outside the Trans-Lux Theater on the corner of New York's 52nd Street and Lexington Avenue. Thousands turned up to watch the scene being shot over and over again.

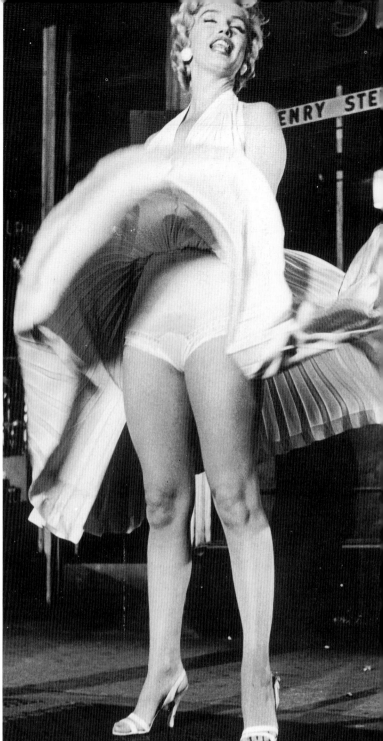

These pages: Joe DiMaggio turned up to watch the filming of the skirt-billowing scene and, by all accounts, was less than amused by his wife's antics in front of the assembled crowd. Whatever the truth of the matter, he and Marilyn were soon to be divorced.

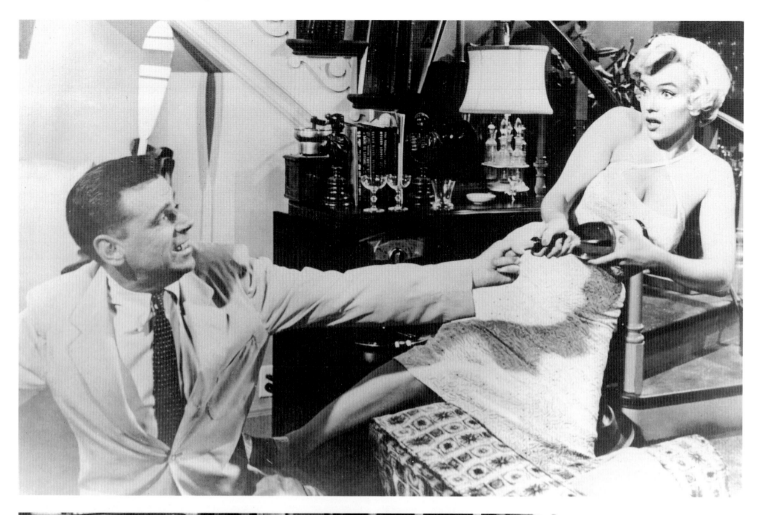

These pages: Marilyn and Tom Ewell enjoy a champagne and potato chips snack during a scene from *The Seven Year Itch*.

These pages: *The Seven Year Itch* was perhaps made at the height of Marilyn's fame. It may not be her best comedy (most would nominate *Some Like It Hot*) but it was made at the end of a five-year period that had seen Marilyn emerge from obscurity on to the world stage.

These pages: In *The Seven Year Itch* Wilder described Marilyn's performance as having 'flesh impact ... when she was on screen there was never a hole.'

These pages: Shooting scenes for *The Seven Year Itch* in New York and the studio.

These pages: Marilyn
vamps it up much to the
delight of *Seven Year Itch*
co-star Tom Ewell.

Above left: Marilyn in the gown she wore in the film *Clash By Night*.

Above: A publicity still from the mid-1950s.

Left: Marilyn enjoying a joke with columnist Walter Winchell.

Right: Marilyn is escorted to Madison Square Garden to perform in a benefit for actors, 1955.

PART 4
The Marilyn Method
1956-59

For all that *The Seven Year Itch* was a huge critical success, Twentieth-Century Fox were still reluctant to accede to Marilyn's wishes about her film roles. It was this state of affairs that led her in 1955 to move to New York. She and the photographer Milton Greene held a press conference to announce the formation of Marilyn Monroe Productions, 'So I can play the better kind of roles I want to play,' Marilyn declared. A further development was her discovery of Lee and Paula Strasberg's Actors' Studio, the acting academy which taught 'The Method.' As Natasha Lytess before her, Paula Strasberg was to serve as the 'strong woman' figure to Marilyn up until her death.

Moving East also represented a radical upheaval in Marilyn's personal life. She had been divorced from DiMaggio in November 1955, and in January 1956 the playwright Arthur Miller also announced he and his wife were to divorce. The official line was that Marilyn was not the cause, but she and Miller were married in July 1956. Miller and DiMaggio could hardly have presented a greater contrast – Marilyn and he were described as the 'Hourglass and the Egghead' – but Marilyn was clearly head-over-ears in love with Miller.

As a further expression of the 'new Marilyn' and, perhaps, as a jib at Hollywood, Marilyn announced in February 1956 that her next film was to be filmed in England with Sir Laurence Olivier. This brought an almost instantaneous offer from Fox of a new contract which only required her to make four films over the next seven years. For each of these she would receive $100,000 and she was also given power of veto over the story, director, cameraman, and makeup man. Significantly, as well as paying for her maid, acting coach, and secretary, Fox also agreed to stump up for Marilyn to visit an analyst. Marilyn was already by this time regularly visiting an analyst. In spite of her superstardom she was often depressed, uncertain, and lonely. She was, moreover, ever-aware of her family history of mental instability.

Before she went to England to film *The Prince and the Showgirl* with Olivier, Marilyn starred as Cherie in *Bus Stop* (1956) for Fox. Cherie is a saloon-singer with whom an enthusiastic Montana cow-

These pages: 'The Hourglass and the
Egghead' – Marilyn and Arthur Miller were
wed on June 29 1956 and, as these pictures
clearly show, were very much in love.

boy (Don Murray) falls in love when he arrives in town for a rodeo. Director Joshua Logan who had had doubts before shooting of Marilyn's ability, was saying by the end, 'I found her to be one of the greatest talents of all time . . . the most constantly exciting actress I ever worked with.' The critics also, for the first time, acknowledged Marilyn's acting skills and not just her physical attributes. Certainly, although far from being her most famous role, Marilyn's Cherie is considered by many to be her finest performance, the role which truly demonstrated her dramatic skills.

She had a much less happy time in England making *The Prince and the Showgirl*. Olivier grew very impatient of Marilyn's unpunctuality and was exasperated by the number of retakes that were necessary. The film, which Olivier directed as well

as starring in opposite Marilyn, was a critical failure in the United States, but it won Marilyn the equivalent of a Best Foreign Actress award in France and Italy.

The year 1957 was to be professionally fallow for Marilyn. She found herself embroiled in the McCarthy witch-hunts when her husband was tried by the house Un-American Activities Committee, and she lost a desperately wanted baby. 1958, however, saw her working on one of her most popular films, *Some Like it Hot* (1959), with Tony Curtis and Jack Lemmon. Although director Billy Wilder found her depressed and difficult to work with on this film, on March 8th 1960, she was awarded the Golden Globe award as Best Actress for her portrayal of Sugar Kane, a member of a (supposedly!) all-girl band.

Left: Marilyn and Miller attend the inaugural meeting of the Watergate Theatre at London's Comedy Theatre, September 9th, 1956.

Above: The fisherman and the mermaid? Miller and Marilyn on holiday.

Right: One of a series of delightful studio shots of Marilyn taken by Milton Greene in 1956.

These pages: *Bus Stop*, widely regarded as Marilyn's best serious acting role, was her first film for Twentieth-Century Fox after signing a new contract with the studio.

These pages: Marilyn
played Cherie, a second-
rate saloon-singer in *Bus
Stop*; her rendition of an
almost tuneless 'That Old
Black Magic' is one of the
film's true high spots.

165

Bus Stop takes places in a rodeo town
in which a simple cowboy meets a
saloon-singer (Marilyn) and asks her
to marry him. Although primarily a
drama, the film also has a lighter,
comical touch in parts.

These pages: Marilyn make-up for the part of Cherie in *Bus Stop* was created by Milton Greene and deliberately gave her a pasty complexion.

These pages: *Bus Stop* was directed
for Twentieth-Century Fox by Joshua
Logan, who also directed *South
Pacific, Camelot* and *Paint Your
Wagon*. The film was photographed
by Milton Krasner.

These pages: To enhance her performance as Cherie, Marilyn was fitted out in a suitably appalling fish-net costume. Film critics were impressed with her performance.

These pages: Marilyn rejects the
amorous advances of Bo, the naive
young cowboy in *Bus Stop*.

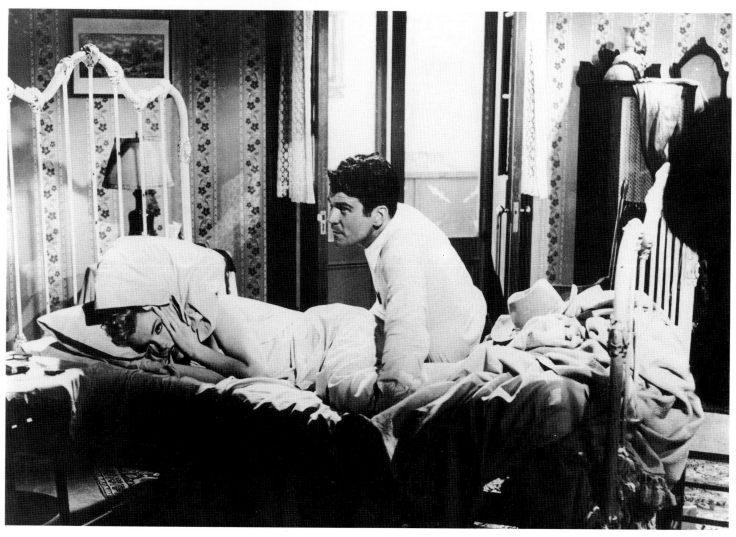

These pages: *Bus Stop* saw Marilyn's acting reach a new level of ability. She now had Paula Strasberg from the famed Actors Studio as her coach rather than Natasha Lytess.

These pages: The rodeo scenes from *Bus Stop* were just one of the film's memorable dramatic highlights produced by Logan's top-rate directing and Marilyn's superb acting.

These pages: The critics were
stunned by Marilyn's abilities in *Bus
Stop*. Their comments included: 'The
girl is a terrific comedienne . . . a
revelation'; 'Marilyn Monroe has
finally proved herself an actress.'

These pages: Although *Bus Stop*
confirmed Marilyn's stardom, it
appears she was having increasing
difficulty in coping with the status
and glare of publicity. Logan had to
deal with her tantrums and frequent
non-appearance on the set.

These pages: In the summer of 1956,
Miller and Marilyn traveled to London
in order to set up a deal with
Lawrence Olivier for the film *The
Prince and the Showgirl*.

These pages: Marilyn and Miller
enjoy the countryside during their
sojourn in England. The pictures
were taken on August 13th, 1956.

Left: Marilyn and Miller attend the first night of his play *A View from the Bridge* at London's Comedy Theatre in early October 1956. Also present are actors Anthony Quayle and Ian Bannen, and director Peter Brook.

Right: Marilyn and Laurence Olivier announce their forthcoming venture *The Prince and the Showgirl* at a press conference in London's Savoy Hotel, July 15 1956.

Right: Marilyn is presented to Queen Elizabeth II before the first night of the film *The Battle of the River Plate* at the Empire Theatre, October 29th, 1956.

Below: Police protection for Marilyn and Miller as they attend London's Lyric Theatre on July 18th, 1956.

This page: Marilyn and
Miller return to the states
after completing *The Prince
and the Showgirl*. They are
seen off by Laurence
Olivier and Vivien Leigh.

This page: Marilyn and Miller attend the opening of *The Prince and the Showgirl* at Radio City on June 13th, 1957.

Above: Marilyn pictured outside her
home in Connecticut.

Left: Olivier and Marilyn in a scene from *The Prince and the Showgirl*.

Below left: Marilyn prepares to shoot a scene from *The Prince and the Showgirl*, originally entitled *The Sleeping Prince*.

Below: Marilyn pictured in 1956.

This page: Marilyn and Olivier give a press conference about their collaboration on *The Prince and the Showgirl.*

This page: In *The Prince and the Showgirl*, Marilyn plays a chorus girl who meets a Ruritanian prince (Olivier). Although from different ends of the social spectrum the pair gradually grow to understand each other.

This page: Marilyn preparing to shoot scenes for *The Prince and the Showgirl*. On hand to help the star (above, left and right) is director of photography Jack Cardiff.

These pages: Marilyn
meets her prince – with
devastating consequences.

These pages: *The Prince and the Showgirl* was based on the play *The Sleeping Prince* by Terrence Rattigan and was directed by Olivier himself.

These pages: *The Prince and the Showgirl* did not meet with critical acclaim in England or the US, but Marilyn was awarded the Italian and French equivalents of an Oscar for her performance in the film.

These pages: It seems that Olivier
and Marilyn did not hit it off while
filming *The Prince and the Showgirl*.
Her lateness on set, among other
things, angered Olivier; Marilyn
thought he lacked sensitivity.

Left: Marilyn attends a grand ball, a scene from *The Prince and the Showgirl*.

Above, above left and left: Olivier and Marilyn together in *The Prince and the Showgirl*. Interestingly, and despite all of the problems encountered, *The Prince and the Showgirl* was one of only two Marilyn movies to fall within budget; the other being *Bus Stop*.

These pages: The
Ruritanian prince and the
showgirl getting to know
each other.

Left: Olivier and Marilyn in a publicity still for *The Prince and the Showgirl*.

Right: Flanked by Milton Greene (left) and Jack Warner, Marilyn announces her part in *The Prince and the Showgirl*, February 1956.

Right: Smiling and evidently relaxed, Marilyn poses for the camera.

These pages: *Some Like It Hot* is widely considered to be Marilyn's finest picture. Also starring Jack Lemmon and Tony Curtis, it begins with the two male leads accidently witnessing the St Valentine's Day Massacre (top right). To avoid tangling with the Mob, Curtis and Lemmon disguise themselves as women.

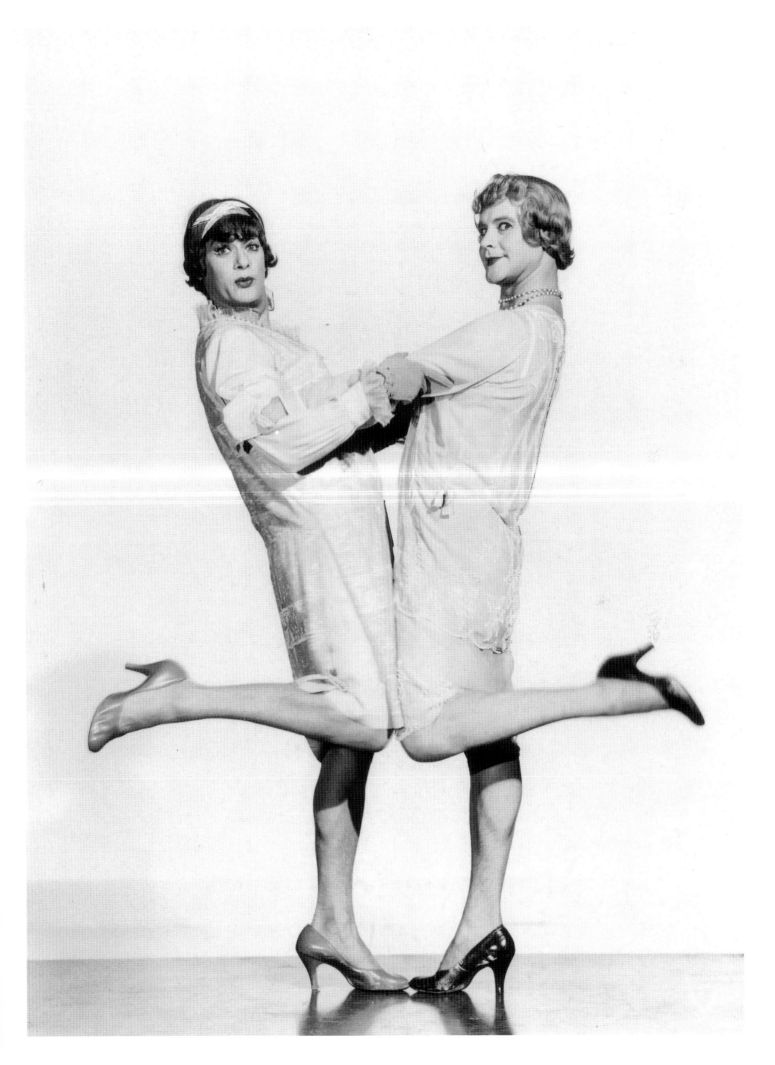

These pages: Pursued by police and villains, Lemmon and Curtis join Sweet Sue's Society Syncopaters to escape – Curtis played tenor sax, Lemmon double bass and Marilyn the ukelele.

These pages: Sweet Sue's Society Syncopaters settle down for the night in the train's sleeping car. Lemmon and Curtis plan a cosy drinking session with Sugar Kane (Marilyn), only to have their plans thwarted by the rest of the band.

Overleaf: Exit Marilyn pursued by Jack Lemmon.

These pages: Marilyn preparing for a scene in *Some Like It Hot*. In this case (above), Marilyn explains to Josephine (Tony Curtis) that she had recently quit playing in an all-male band because she fell in love with its sax player.

Above and right: Sweet Sue's Society Syncopaters, including Marilyn and Jack Lemmon, enjoy the pleasures of the beach.

Right: In order to woo Marilyn, Tony Curtis disguises himself as a vacationing millionaire, complete with an accent reminiscent of Cary Grant, much to the chagrin of Jack Lemmon.

These pages: While Josephine chases
Sugar Kane, Jack Lemmon also finds
a suitor – an aging millionaire.
Despite the sparkling performances of
all concerned Curtis and Marilyn
could not stand acting together.

This page: Curtis attempts to woo Marilyn by inviting her aboard 'his' private yacht moored off the resort. He is unsuccessful!

Above: Marilyn had three singing
numbers in *Some Like It Hot*:
'Running Wild,' 'I'm Through With
Love' and 'I Want To Be Loved
By You.'

These pages: Marilyn preparing for shooting a scene for *Some Like It Hot* with Arthur Miller, her costumier and taking time out to sign autographs.

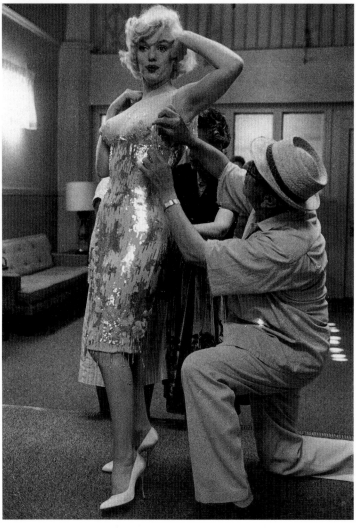

This page: The Mob arrives at the Miami Hotel where Sweet Sue's Society Syncopaters are in residency. The head gangster is played by the magnificent George Raft.

This page: Lemmon and Curtis, fearing for their lives, attempt to escape the clutches of the Mob.

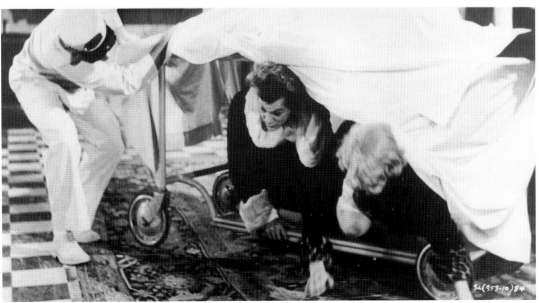

These pages: *Some Like It Hot* was directed by the talented Billy Wilder and is widely recognized as a comedy classic, although relations on the set were fraught. Marilyn had a miscarriage during filming and her relationship with Arthur Miller seems to have been deteriorating.

Something's Got to Give

1960-62

When Marilyn and Yves Montand began work on the film *Let's Make Love*, trouble was brewing in her marriage to Miller. Marilyn was having an affair with Montand which ended sadly for Marilyn when he backed away at the publicity their liaison was attracting. Nonetheless her next film was to be scripted by Miller. *The Misfits* is the story of two women who fall in with a group of cowboys played by Clark Gable, Eli Wallach, and Montgomery Clift. Miller drew extensively on his experiences of Marilyn from their life together and her character Roslyn has many of her own attributes – loneliness, vulnerability, and distaste for cruelty to animals. The film also provided Marilyn with the opportunity to work with her hero Clark Gable.

The progress of the film was far from smooth. Tension between Miller and Marilyn was high as they were drifting apart, and Marilyn was relying more and more on alcohol and pills to see her through each day. Eventually she was taken off to hospital suffering from 'acute exhaustion.' More-

over, the strain and heat of the Nevada location were too much for Gable, who died of a heart attack shortly after shooting ended. The same month, November 1960, Marilyn announced that her marriage to Miller was over.

Despite the critical acclaim that greeted both her own and Clark Gable's performances, Marilyn was so emotionally distressed that in March 1961 her psychiatrist placed her in the Payne Whitney Psychiatric Clinic in New York. She now found herself, as she had dreaded, behind bars and locked windows. Finally she persuaded Joe DiMaggio to prevail upon the authorities to let her go.

In stark contrast to this private despair, Marilyn was awarded the Golden Globe award of 1962 as the world's most popular star. In April she began work on another film, titled prophetically, *Something's Got to Give*, directed by George Cukor. Although Marilyn had approved the script, Cukor made constant changes which she could not cope with. After failing to turn up once too often,

These pages: After *Some Like It Hot*, Marilyn's next project was entitled *Let's Make Love*. Marilyn's co-star was Yves Montand who is pictured far left (centre) with Arthur Miller, Montand's wife Simone Signoret, and Frankie Vaughan.

Marilyn was sacked by Cukor from the film.

One reason for Marilyn's many absences from the set of *Something's Got to Give* was her increasingly intimate relationship with both Bobby and John F Kennedy. At one point she had flown during the filming to New York to sing 'Happy Birthday, Mr President,' at a JFK birthday party. Although he seems to have cooled off their affair, during July Marilyn seems to have made repeated attempts to contact his brother Bobby at the Department of Justice. Like so many before him, it seems that he too now rejected Marilyn.

On August 5th, 1962 the world learnt that Marilyn Monroe had taken her own life. Many suspicious occurences after her death, including discrepancies of evidence have fueled speculation of a

cover-up, even that she was murdered, perhaps as part of the same tangle of events that were to lead to John F Kennedy's own death a year later.

These pages: Marilyn (seen, left, with Frankie Vaughan) was unhappy with the original script of *Let's Make Love* and asked Arthur Miller to rewrite it. Gregory Peck, Cary Grant, Charlton Heston and Rock Hudson all turned down the male lead. Montand was signed up after Marilyn had seen his one-man show on Broadway.

These pages: *Let's Make Love* concerns a billionaire (Montand) who, hearing that he is the butt of jokes in an off-Broadway revue, goes to a rehearsal and is hired to play himself. He meets and then falls in love with Marilyn.

These pages: *Let's Make Love* was directed by George Cukor, who was also responsible for *The Philadelphia Story* and *My Fair Lady*. Both he and Montand would become increasingly irritated by Marilyn's lack of punctuality and frequent 'illnesses' during shooting.

These pages: Marilyn sang several songs in *Let's Make Love*, including 'Incurably Romantic,' 'Let's Make Love' and 'Specialization.'

Previous pages: Perhaps the best remembered number in the film was Marilyn's version of Cole Porter's classic 'My Heart Belongs To Daddy.'

These pages: Marilyn, Montand and George Cukor run through a scene from *Let's Make Love*.

Pages 248-249: Marilyn rehearsing a song and dance number for the film. The tight-fitting costume reveals that she was slightly overweight for the film.

These pages: Marilyn and Frankie
Vaughan in one of the song-and-
dance numbers from *Let's Make
Love*. Despite the number of stars
making cameo appearances in the
film, few critics could find anything
complimentary to say about it.

These pages: The filming of *Let's Make Love* generated a great deal of gossip, most notably about the close relationship between Marilyn and Montand. A liaison was broken off by Montand much to Marilyn's despair.

These pages: Despite hiring Gene Kelly to teach him to dance, Bing Crosby to sing and Milton Berle to be funny, Montand's character remained unconvincing in the film.

These pages: *Let's Make Love*, widely seen as one of Marilyn's poorer films, ended a run of outstanding successes and, in retrospect, can be viewed as marking a decisive downturn in both her personal and professional life.

These pages: The relationship between Montand and Marilyn did not survive the filming of *Let's Make Love*; Montand returned to his wife while Marilyn resumed her marriage with Miller.

These pages: Following the less-than-brilliant *Let's Make Love*, Marilyn's next project was the drama *The Misfits*. Scripted by Miller it offered Marilyn a serious and challenging role alongside several Hollywood legends.

These pages: *The Misfits*, directed by the great John Huston, concerns a disparate group of cowboys who gather together in the Nevada desert to rope wild mustangs. They are joined by a divorcee, Rosyln, played by Marilyn.

These pages: Leading actress, scriptwriter and director – Marilyn, Miller and Huston – discuss a scene during the filming of *The Misfits*.

These pages: In one sense at least,
The Misfits was a dream come true
for Marilyn in that she was able to
work with one of her favorite stars –
Clark Gable.

Following pages: Marilyn and Gable
together in *The Misfits*. Although
acting in temperature of over 100° in
the desert, Marilyn was marvelous
playing a vulnerable character
looking for love and affection.

These pages: Aside from Gable,
The Misfits also starred Eli Wallach
(above, second from right) and
Montgomery Clift (far right).

These pages: The filming of *The Misfits* was fraught with major difficulties: Marilyn and Miller's marriage appeared to be on the rocks and Marilyn was relying heavily on a mixture of alcohol and prescription drugs. Indeed, filming was halted at one stage for two weeks after Marilyn was rushed to Westside Hospital in Los Angeles to have her stomach pumped.

Above: Marilyn and Miller in
lighthearted mood.

Right: Marilyn – still the
'little girl lost.'

These pages: Joe DiMaggio
accompanies Marilyn after
her divorce from Miller.
DiMaggio, always a friend
to Marilyn, rescued her
from the Payne Whitney
Psychiatric Clinic in New
York, which Marilyn had
entered for a period of rest
and consultation shortly
after filming *The Misfits*.

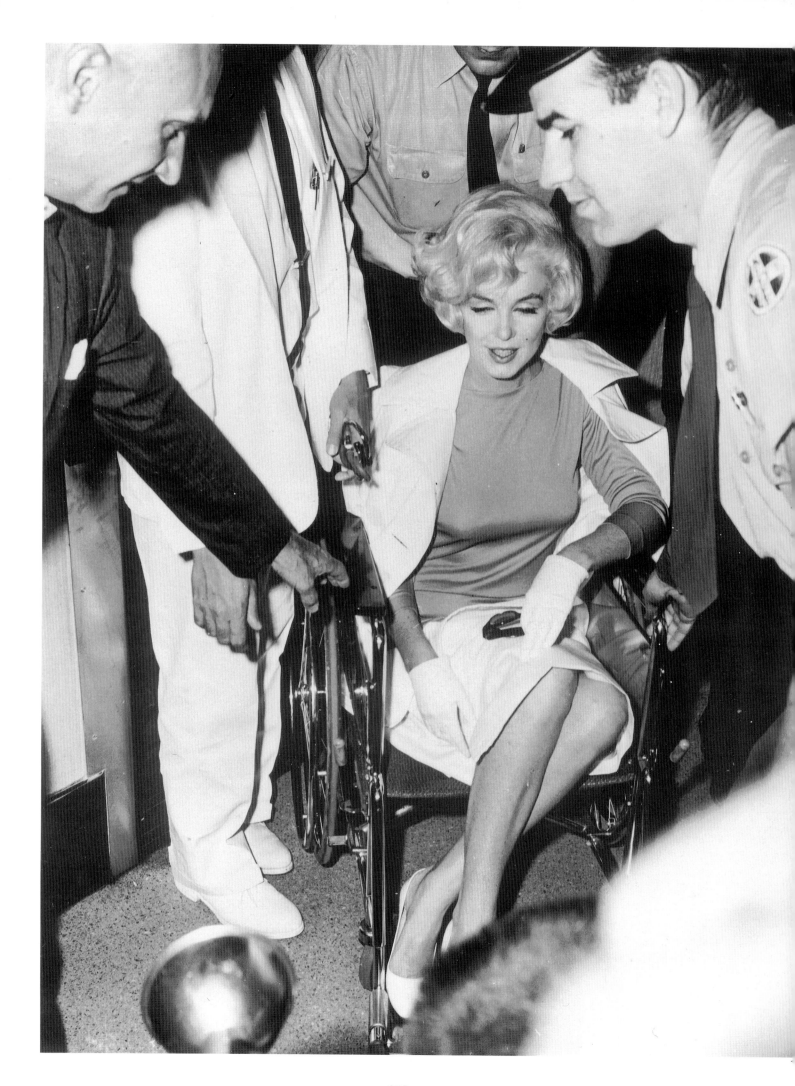

These pages: A clearly
unwell Marilyn leaves
hospital on 3 May 1961.
This time in Los Angeles.

These pages: Seemingly recovered from her various ailments, Marilyn began shooting her final film, *Something's Got To Give*, a remake of a Cary Grant film, *My Favorite Wife*, released in 1940. Sadly, the remake was finally released in 1963 as *Move Over, Darling*, starring Doris Day.

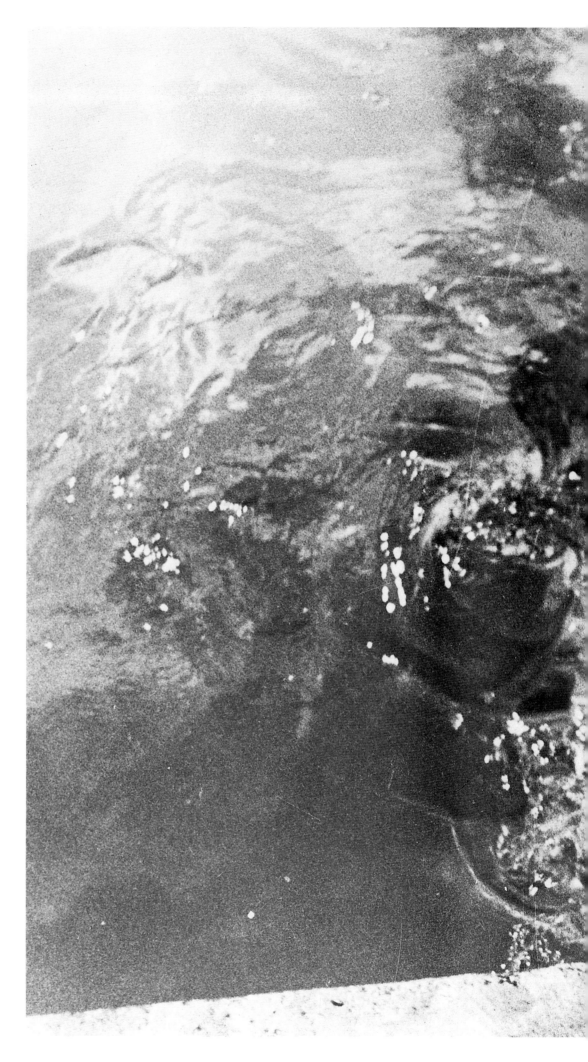

Left: Rock Hudson
congratulates Marilyn on
winning the Golden Globe
award for being a 'world
film favorite,' 1961.

Above: Marilyn and
admirers at the Golden
Globe ceremony.

Right: Marilyn enjoys a
glass of champagne on the
night of the awards.

Above: Marilyn and her Mexican
lover, Jose Bolanos, pictured in 1962.

Right: Marilyn looking a little the
worse for wear.

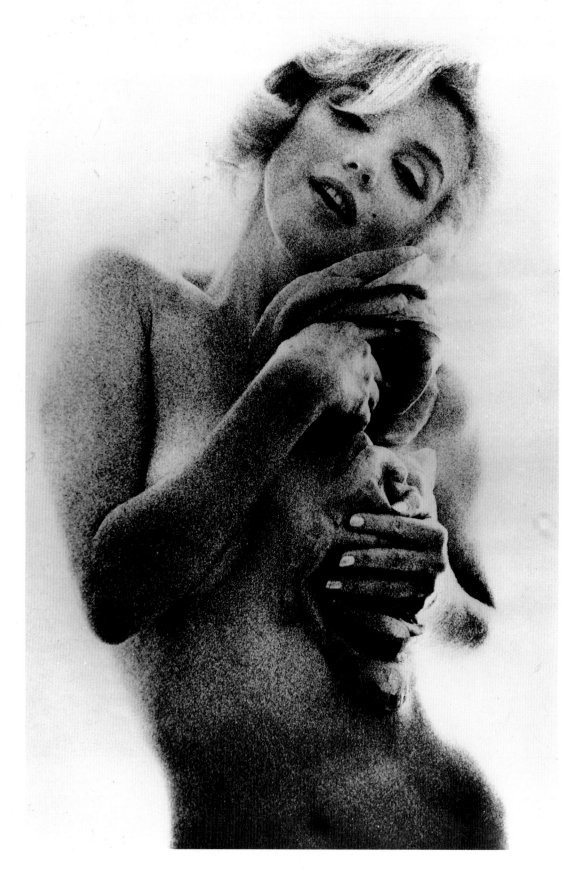

These pages: Photographs taken by
Bert Stern in June 1962. They were
later released in his book *The Last
Sitting.*

Marilyn Monroe: "I was never used to being happy."

THE MONROE SAGA: 7 PAGES OF STORIES AND PICTURES

These pages: Marilyn died on
August 5th, 1962. Her body was
discovered at her home on
Fifth Helena Drive, Brentwood,
California.

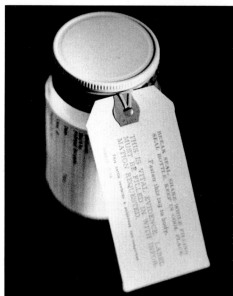

Top: Marilyn's home in Brentwood.

Above: Evidence relating to the death of Marilyn Monroe – a bottle filled with her stomach contents.

Left, below left, below and overleaf: The funeral of Monroe, with Joe DiMaggio and his son (in Marine uniform) in attendance.

297

Marilyn – the beauty and
the tragedy.

INDEX

Acknowledgments

The author and publisher would like to thank Ian Westwell who captioned this book, Ann Lloyd, Neil Sinyard, and Anthony Summers, for the inspiration of their writings on Marilyn, and the following institutions, individuals, and agencies for providing the illustrations:

Academy of Motion Picture Arts and Sciences: pages 57 (top right), 58 (bottom), 67 (bottom right), 74, (top), 108 (top), 109, 110-111, 134 (top), 144 (right), 162, 172 (bottom left and right)

Bettmann Archive, New York: page 164 (bottom left)

Brompton Books: pages 5, 94 (right), 161 (bottom), 290, 291, 300

British Film Institute, Posters, Films and Stills, London: pages 41 (bottom), 42 (bottom left), 52 (top), 55 (top), 56, 57 (top left and bottom), 58 (top), 60-61 (all 3), 62 (bottom), 64-65 (all 3), 66 (bottom), 67 (top left), 68 (top and bottom left), 72-73 (all 7), 74 (bottom left and right), 75 (both), 77, (both), 78, 79, ;80-81 (all 6), 82 (all 4), 83 (top and bottom left), 84-85 (all 4), 86-87 (all 7), 88-89 (all 3), 90 (all 3), 92-93 (all 6), 94 (top right), 95 (both), 96-97 (all three), 98-99 (all three), 100-101 (all 4), 102-103 (all 3), 104-105 (all 4), 106-107 (all 3), 108 (bottom left), 110, 111, 124 (both), 126-127 (all 5), 128 (both), 129 (left), 131, 132-33 (all 3), 134 (bottom), 135 (bottom), 136, 138-39 (all 5), 146-47 (all 3), 148-49 (all 3), 150-51 (all 3), 152 (top left and bottom), 154-55 (all 3), 163, 164 (top and bottom right), 165 (both), 166-67 (all 4), 169 (bottom), 170-71 (all 4), 173 (both), 174-75 (all 3), 176 (top left and bottom), 177 (all 3), 178-79 (all 3), 180-81 (all 3), 182-83 (all 4), 192-93 (all 3), 194 (top and bottom left), 195 (top and middle), 196-97 (all 6), 198-99 (all 6), 200-201 (all 4), 202-203 (all 4), 204-205 (all 3), 206-207 (all 6), 208-209 (all 3), 210, 211 (top), 212-213 (all 5), 215 (below left and right), 216-217 (all 4), 222 (both), 223 (bottom right), 224 (top left and right), 226 (top, bottom left, and right), 230-231 (all 7), 233 (bottom left), 234, 238-39 (all 4), 240 (top), 241 (top left), 242-43 (all 6), 244-45 (all 3), 250-51 (all 5), 253 (top left, top right, and right), 254 (all 3), 256-57 (all 4), 258 (top), 260 (top left and right), 262-63 (all 3), 264-65 (all 3), 267, 268-69 (all 3), 270-71 (all 3), 272-73 (all 4), 274-75 (all 3), 276-77, 279, 284, 302

The Hulton-Deutsch Collection, London: pages 1, 31 (top left), 120, 122, 123, 135 (top), 184-85 (all 3), 186-87 (both), 188-89 (all 6), 190-91 (all 5), 241 (top right), 252, 282-83 (both), 288

Kobal Collection: page 17

Pictorial Press Ltd, London: pages 2-3, 4, 6, 7, 8 (both), 9, 10, 11 (top), 12-13 (all 4), 14-15 (all 3), 20-21 (all 5), 23 (all 3), 24, 25, 26 (both), 27, 28-29 (all 6), 30 (both), 31 (top right and bottom), 32-33 (all 5), 34-35 (all 4), 36-37 (all 4), 38, 39, 40 (all 3), 41 (top), 42 (top and bottom right), 43 (both), 44 (all 3), 46-47 (all 4), 49, 50-51 (all 3), 52 (bottom), 53 (both), 54, 55 (bottom), 59 (both), 62 (top), 63, 66 (top left and right), 67 (top right and bottom left), 68 (bottom right), 69, 70-71 (all 3), 76, 83 (top right and bottom right), 91, 94 (left), 108 (bottom right), 112-113 (both), 114, 115, 116-17 (all 3), 118, 119, 121, 125, 129 (right), 130, 137, 140-41, 142-43 (both), 144 (left), 145 (all 3), 152 (top right), 153, 156-57 (all 4), 158-59 (all 3), 160, 161 (top), 168, 169 (top left and right), 172 (top), 176 (top right), 194 (bottom right), 195 (bottom), 211 (bottom), 214, 215 (top), 218-19 (all 3), 220-21 (all 3), 223 (top and bottom left), 224 (bottom), 225 (both, 226 (center right), 227 (both), 228-29 (all 4, 232, 233 (top, center right, and bottom right), 235 (both), 236-37 (all 5), 240 (bottom), 241 (bottom), 246-47 (all 4), 248-49 (all 5), 253 (center right and bottom right), 255, 258 (bottom), 259, 260 (bottom), 261, 266 (both), 278, 280-81 (all 3), 285 (both), 286-87, 288 (both), 292-93 (both), 294-95 (both), 296-97 (all 5), 298-99, 300-301

Vintage Magazine Company: pages 22, 48

Bill Yenne: pages 11 (bottom), 45
George Zeno Collection: pages 16, 18, 19